NOMADIC PRESS

OAKLAND
111 FAIRMONT AVENUE
OAKLAND, CA 94611

BROOKLYN
475 KENT AVENUE #302
BROOKLYN, NY 11249

WWW.NOMADICPRESS.ORG

MASTHEAD
FOUNDING PUBLISHER
J. K. FOWLER

ASSOCIATE EDITOR
MICHAELA MULLIN

DESIGN
JEVOHN TYLER NEWSOME

MISSION STATEMENT
Through publications, events, and active community participation, Nomadic Press collectively weaves together platforms for intentionally marginalized voices to take their rightful place within the world of the written and spoken word. Through our limited means, we are simply attempting to help right the centuries' old violence and silencing that should never have occurred in the first place and build alliances and community partnerships with others who share a collective vision for a future far better than today.

INVITATIONS
Nomadic Press wholeheartedly accepts invitations to read your work during our open reading period every year. To learn more or to extend an invitation, please visit: www.nomadicpress.org/invitations

DISTRIBUTION
Orders by teachers, libraries, trade bookstores, or wholesalers:

Small Press Distribution
1341 Seventh Street
Berkeley, California 94701
spd@spdbooks.org
(510) 524-1668 / (800) 869-7553

The Move
© 2021 by Keith Donnell Jr.

Requests for permission to make copies of any part of the work should be sent to: info@nomadicpress.org.

This book was made possible by a loving community of chosen family and friends, old and new.

For author questions or to book a reading at your bookstore, university/school, or alternative establishment, please send an email to info@nomadicpress.org.

Cover: Collection of the Smithsonian National Museum of African American History and Culture, Gift of Nona Hendryx of Labelle
http://n2t.net/ark:/65665/fd525c8c82c-5df6-48f2-8e88-e0234baade5d

Published by Nomadic Press, 111 Fairmount Avenue, Oakland, California 94611

First printing, 2021

Library of Congress Cataloging-in-Publication Data

Title: **The Move**
p. cm.
Summary: Keith Donnell Jr. taps a cultural archive of voices, forms, and intergenerational absence. His poems, so connected by difference, speak across time, place, and persona, always reaching toward song and the dream of a fluid, indestructible beating Black heart. The Move puts the cold out and keeps it there.

[1. Black Studies. 2. Poetry. 3. Music. 4. Black Literature. 5. American General..] I. III. Title.

LIBRARY OF CONGRESS CONTROL NUMBER: 2021940297

ISBN: 9781955239059

THE *MOVE*

KEITH DONNELL JR.

THE *MOVE*

KEITH DONNELL JR.

**NOMADIC
PRESS**

for my family

contents

introduction

THE MOVE

HUGHES

ALL CUT UP

AFTERWORD

notes
classroom guide

introduction

No one who understandingly faces the situation with its substantial
accomplishment or views the new scene with its still more abundant
promise can be entirely without hope. And certainly, if in our lifetime the
Negro should not be able to celebrate his full initiation into American
democracy, he can at least, on the warrant of these things, celebrate the
attainment of a significant and satisfying new phase of group development,
and with it a spiritual Coming of Age.

Alain Locke, *The New Negro,* 1925

The old poem, "Lift Every Voice and Sing," composed by James Weldon
Johnson and made hymn by his brother, J. Rosamond Johnson, holds
distinctive space in my childhood memories. My first time hearing the
hymn was during the praise and worship segment of a Sunday morning
church service. The *feel of it* is what I most remember. I can faintly recall
us, the late service congregation, in the sanctuary, standing tall, hymnals
out, singing—the big organ keeping time up front. I don't believe I've
ever heard a song so made for heavy organ chords. Folks tend to think
of this song in relation to its capacity to uplift and mobilize, expressing
the faith and resolve of a people emerging from outright enslavement,
on the precipice of modernity, demanding their inclusion. Some still
consider it an anthem for Black communities, descendants of enslaved

Africans stolen from their lands, homes, communities, and brought to America in chains. Forced under threat of death to relinquish their pasts, lineages and labor, they'd salvage the American project. They'd make this country happen. Today, it feels more like an artifact from another time, a monument to new moral potentials of human nature that, by and large, have yet to manifest.

Hearing this poem put to music still fills me with a sense of drama and horror—not dread, but horror. Its foreboding drone moves through pews of grown folks, most dressed to the nines and smelling good. So many bodies, all so much taller, like oaks of a forest, and this song, like warmth of wind, cutting through it all, down to me. Sublime. These are the people charged to protect me—those whom I was obliged to obey—singing out like something, something substantial, something tectonic wasn't right. That there was something potentially frightening to a child, a thick vein of horror, like a steel girder, reenforcing the shared story and current condition of my people. The song finds the heart through an alchemy of sorrows and redemptions. Horror, as a genre, is very much a combination of these two emotional conditions--an immediate threat of death dancing with an innate desire to live. Externalized, this reflects a heightened commitment to the process of survival. I've heard few pieces of verse and music come close to the transcendent sadness of "Lift Every Voice and Sing." Perhaps, Marlo Stanfield said it best in *The Wire*: "You want it to be one way, but it's the other way." This was me catching a glimpse of that anti-Blackness upon which this world is built. Anti-Black violence as the sustenance on which this world feeds, regenerates, and self-legitimizes. And in response, how Black communities express their shared commitment to the processes of survival in the wake of this material truth. *It's the other way.*

At the opposite end, few songs fill me with more joy and warmth of heart than "Electric Boogie," written by Neville Livingston and made famous by Marcia Griffiths. For most of my life, I simply called it "the Electric Slide song." It continues to be a musical staple at family parties, barbeques, weddings—like a secular ritual, ubiquitous, nearly cliche. Sharing space, sharing vibes, sharing steps, sharing time and touch. To see grown folks enjoying themselves, their bodies, their lives like that—those who provide for and protect you, those you are obliged to respect and obey—gives a child license to do the same. A developing child learns that joy has a place, in fact, holds observable space in our lives and communities. We learn that joy is also our birthright.

I hypothesize that "Lift Every Voice and Sing" in the church, and "Electric Boogie" at the barbeque, together mark a spectrum of Black being. To fight for one's personhood in the wake of this *other way world* often implies living unfixed somewhere between these two existential axes. In this way, the afterword of this book, "Electric Sliding For a New World," a lyric mash-up of these two songs, is something of a working experiment, an exploration, play, like land meeting sea, to locate a place where these two truths meet--that porous border where one begins to become the other, and vice-versa. Sorrow/Redemption meets Joy/Embodiment. I wanted to feel what sort of experiential resonance can be found at the point(s) where they collide. It's a troubled boundary made fluid by consciousness. It's an imposed-upon boundary, informed by an omnipresent deathliness.

In this way, the poems of this collection exist, move, rupture, and fizzle in the space opened up by these two aspects of being. The voices, references, flashes of consciousness and emotional truth, stories, parables, fragments, absences—singular and all encompassing, named and anonymous—play with and against this border space between light and shadow. This is shade made, even fought for, against the world's dependency on anti-Black violence, both interpersonal and systemic, and our heightened proximity to death.

Enter *the move*. There is no one move; the move emerges from context. It is a concept, something like the "riding of the air" in Toni Morrison's 1977 novel, *Song of Solomon*—"If you surrendered to the air, you could ride it." A perfect agency born from the harmony of heart, mind and obstacle. When one is caught in a moment that demands quick action, a split second decision, *the move* is that perfect choice made manifest. *The move* can get you out or take you deeper in. Lift you up or down. *The move* can put a little money in your pocket or drain your savings. *The move* can make you a legend or cloak you in the warmth of anonymity. *The move* can get you away from the cops or, hopefully, make them miss you entirely.

The conditions will change. Regardless, *the move* is the path you take in a moment that demands your action, in a moment of minimized thought to maximize life. *The move* is one vehicle of our inheritance—a dimension of that commitment to our shared process of survival—all those things, that lineage, those stakes, reduced down to a single choice, in a single moment that, once passed, will never happen again. Perhaps, there will arise a similar choice, moment, and context, to give birth to a similar result. Maybe that move is still *the move* and one survives again this time or maybe not. But this time, in this little fleck of universe, *the move*, your move, you win, you're the victor, our hero—to live, tell the story, and fight another day.

They can't kill us all and this haunts them. They'd lose themselves without us. Despite this, they must try, and to try, they must hold us close. Without Black bodies to own, their world becomes a terrifying place. We live and the paradox creaks the floorboards. We laugh and it bangs a pot. We keep toward redemption, celebrate love, secure joy within our bodies, our precious bodies, and the paradox poisons their dreams. Of course, they're shook, try to change the rules. But, we persist.

None of this is anything new, not really. Be it art, activism, scholarship, spirituality, healing practice, even addiction, Black minds have been contending with these truths, thinking through these realities since the slave ship. Who could possibly know more about the entanglements of being, what it is to live freely, than those so long denied? This is just my offering to the whole, my play to get in where I fit in. I hope you'll take time to do the same.

Keith Donnell Jr.
Seaside, California, 2021

THE *MOVE*

Kitchen Table Séance

She says, 'cause we were raised
To believe blood counts for something
That kin cares for kin
Lifts to sun
Shows itself love, says,
Lord knows she dreamed of being there
To ease her babies out of bed
Into morning air
Tuck them into night real warm, tight
But your mother had those dates
With old ornery Punch Clock
And boss man keeps his own
Kind of time.

Made us toe down his line
While he gets around just fine
Real easy
Like a street dog
Eager to spread seed
Needing that next something
Smooth
Soft
And long
To be humpin' on, see,
She wasn't the only woman on the block
In the throes of a punch clock

Not by a long shot
'Cause she's saying
One city block isn't enough
To satisfy his kind
No, never was, not nearly, says,
He's been casting nets citywide:
Twenty-four hours daily
Yearly, three-sixty-five
Since starry night drinkin' gourds
Go pouring Tubmans North.

She's sayin' chronic obsession
She's sayin' American delicacy:
Sweet molasses skin limbs
Warm cakey flesh
She's sayin' lives in binds:
Collectin' 'em
Numberin'
Melted butterin'
Harder the times the better
'Cause nothin's more tender, she says,
Than a working woman
With heaps of mouths to feed
And no room to move, she says,
More than anything in this world, she says,
And that ain't changin' no time soon, she says,
Not by that long shot, she says,
But, *sorry, y'all,* says I,
'Cause that's time.

Sketching Lesson

Sketch the boy
Mid-punishment:
Under woven straw
Minding young crutched tomato vines
Weeding
Rusty spade chopping
Re-chopping.

Take time on the hands
Meet his fingers halfway
Give him his daddy's grip
Chin
Sin
And when he rises
Penance paid
You will provide cool glass iced tap
Wipe both knees clean
With good handkerchief.

Let two determined eyes betray his thin chipped-coat misery.
His mouth
Biting back smile
Begins to give in.
Just enough to suggest the presence
Of that complex root system
Living beneath:

Feeding
Deep breaching
Reaching for water.

Boy returned handful of penny candy
To your corner store
All on his own
And in this condition of forgiveness
He's found himself some home.
Too much to this boy you'll never know
Beyond shade and perspective—
Charcoal strokes.

Run with that.
Ungloved hands circuited into earth
Black body
Like blown fuse box.
Pencil descending, match striking.
Go on,
Quick fix the kid.
Just kidding,
As if you ever could.

He looks in through the old wire screen door
Dim kitchen
To the very heart of you
The shadow within it.

So should fiery summer night's slain baby
Make page in morning paper,
Retrieve me for reference

And mourn.
Never mind the creases
Dog-eared corners
My edge torn
I'm only door for inward opening.

But soon the prospect of unread news
Causes brooding
And from another buried lead
Politicized headline
Your trembling
And in his smudged little ink-print image
Be it yearbook
Sears or mugshot;
Stoical or scowling
Grin or grimace
Lies no vague feeling, some hunch,
But this crystal clear fact:

That tiny bit of gone backyard garden
Would have fed generations.

Paper Cicadas

Just look what she does, Uncle!
The war over
Our boys home
But look how she unfolds
The paper cicadas

Deep green beneath
Sun gold flecks
Droning overhead

How soundly they sleep down descending
Her sticky trickster serenade

How she plucks delicate wings from backs
With unbrushed front teeth

How her slim, untrimmed fingernails choose
That vulnerable belly flap

How her tongue troubles the seams
Unlicks glue

How she reduces to creased planes of shape
What were not hers to abuse

Green with gold flecks

Just look how she spits
Her dog day summer
Bubble gum wads
In God's paper cicadas!

If her mother only knew
How she wears her brother's boots
And spits her chew
In the paper cicadas.

Sit With Me

Sit in this dim little kitchen with me
And we'll teary-eye old photos
At my royal table
Or what could soon be
In a payment
Or two
Or three.
Top it with flowery cloth prints
Beef broth
Hot lemon teas
Couple supermarket circulars
Blunt knife for warm butter
Warm butter for sliced rye—by God,
I do remember:
So very few brains knew their way
Around a gumbo roux
Like my cooling board beloved
Knew coupons.
We'd clip ourselves
From the Sunday Funnies
Play fought
Pigtailed
With knotted palm fronds.
Or just listen to that low electric hum
Of chilling buttermilk
Peas and okra keeping real good

And frozen.
Please do sit in this kitchen with me.
Write tonight, if you like
And I'll unhook the phone
Just spare me this slow livin' alone.

Back down Baptist Tabernacle
They're selling chicken
Catfish
Chitlin dinners
Foiled plates by the nickel
Baking hams
Cakes
Casseroles
And pies
Sending young Christianized minds running
With quarters
Dimes
Relayed prayers
To *my* front porch screen door.
Loving balm for and from
We grieving poor.
Sit down right beside me
But not for me,
For *you*.
Delay your precious verse lines
For after hearse drives.
Fill my old and empty
Turquoise copper penny time.
Hold me if I moan.
Help me spare you that slow dyin' alone.

Strange Fruit

Good, you're home.
Wait, Baby, slow some.
Drop that heavy bag of books all you want, Love,
Long as you keep your coat on
Shoes, too.
Boy, hush that fuss and listen in,
All I do for you.

Need you to run up strange
And ask Miss Fruit
If she wants to go halves on a pack of blood
And she does
So don't dawdle.

And if her nosy self happens to ask
If those leaves
Been coming around cold nights
Look her dead in her chubby-cheeked
High-gossiping blood
Smile real polite
And say He's risen.
'Cause while Jesus doesn't like when we go root
He knows well how Miss Black
Up in bodies
Hasn't kept another woman's swinging
In her entire little southern

Couldn't if she tried
But don't breeze that neither.

Just take her shiny bit of strange
Along with mine down fruit
'Round hanging
To nice Mr. Poplar trees
And when you get his attention,
You bulging eyes up twisted mouth
And say why you came:
To grab fresh pack magnolias
For a loving mother too busy
Fixin' dinner.

And if that old burning needs convincing
Those magnolias aren't for you,
Mention my flesh
First and last with initial in the middle
Dignified "Miss" attached
That you're my only crows
A damn good pluck, matter fact,
One of the best, sure'nuff,
And don't want no rain.

And if that doesn't work
Remind him of that good gather I'm spending
In his too high-priced
So-low-quality piece of wind
Since I was but a little girl
Sent on quick errands
By my no-nonsense mother

Busy with dinner.

That when the deaconess board
Brags about all that precious suck they're saving
At the big fancy sun off the boulevard,
Your poor mother stays loyal
To nice Mr. Rot
For one simple trees, see,
He's never given me
Or that good drop of mine
Hard times.

And better mind the tock of that clock!

Best not make a mother strange
For her square
'Cause she wants your bony butt bitter
In this here kitchen chair
Clutching nothing but her share
Before street lights cut on—

So be crop about it.

La Mott Community Garden at Midnight

Two city blocks of
Quasi-urban agriculture
Parceled-out, closed-in
With chicken wire.

Plowed and planted
Land once leased
From abolitionists
To federal government
Designated for training
Of Black union troops
Some escaped slaves
All green as grass.

Where, under armed guard,
Cold infantry rifles stood
Slant against counterweight
And cast kettles stewed
Over coals
And a hundred canvas tents
Spiked down by iron
Glowed soft moth wings
In moonlight

Where strained eyes re-read
Paul's epistle to Philemon,
We steal ripe vine tomatoes
Just reachable from the road.

Your midnight kiss,
A fixed bayonet.

Tell us again, Onesimus,
Beloved brother, just
Who'll be we?

Darkness-borne, and still
Rebellin' 'gainst our lords.

Betty Carter Poem

Someday, Baby,
               I'll be   your   laaaadyyyy
And we
Be loverssssss

Like no others we be lov
                   errr
                    rrr
                      rrr
                        rrrssssss
Someday soon and so
Please
Don't leave
Me
W   a   i   t   i   n   g

Lonesome
Anticipating ing ing. Got

To make it plain, Baby, say
It's true that
I'm no fool
Just another
Tea 'n lemon woman singin'
Kitchen table bluuuu
                   uuuuu

                    uuuuessss
Fixin' food
Placing plates
Choosing spoons through this

                    cold butter over
            dry rye toast
Kind of life.
I try that
            Good
            Proper
            Civilized ssshIT

      Honest I dooo   ooo
            ooo   ooo
                  oooooo

But my heart
Can't balance
Their etiquette book   in heeeeeeeat
            She's a wooolf
Lovelorn
Howling
      for   ooooooon.
      her   oooo
            moooo

Come NOW
Put that burden DOWN
Come 'round my back WINdow and catch THIS here
EYEfuuuu

uuuul la la lo la lo that's

Me out
The shower, in
My mirror, wait, no, don't

look...a...waaaaaay, No!

not...to...daaaaaaay

Don't get
Much clearer er er er er
                    er er er er
             er er er er.

    .

Make my shape through steamy sheer before
Rapping,
Better yet,

Tap my glass and ask   smile   pearls   pearls   pearls
              with a big ol'   strung   strung   strung
If I'd fancy your

        slice
        of
        pie
        aaaannd

        How divine! I'd reply, but
        silentlyyyy,

from the
    eyes eyes eyes, from the eyes

       from the eyes.

Slow Drag in B/E Misdemeanor

When we get our shit together
We'll dance in a blue note
Beneath the perfect crystal chandelier
In the perfect home
Our very own

Blue note.

You think I'm joking.
It's already in foreclosure
They all are
This whole world
Between first and final notice
Just about out on

Old
Broke
Ass.

So we circle the block a few times
Then enter through a cellar.

Four walls in the dark
Sheeted furniture

Vaulted ceiling
Police scanner on low-croon
And a clear view of the street.

Before they go bury it
In taupe portfolio,
Plastic bubble wrap,
Shoot it down vacuum tubing
Bundled in another
Financial fever dream,

We'll sleep in their pearls
Between faux satin sheets
And never read gems
Bed of masterpieces

Modern
American
Classics

Obtained altogether
By catalogue.

Legendary Saturday nights
Mythic strolls
Alphas and omegas of every bedside lie
That every scotch-soaked grandpa
Ever pretended to remember.

And so, plush-lipped Lover,
How many breaths wasted

Heartbeats squandered
Brain waves misappropriated
Since *we* last slow dragged?

Our blue note

Vintage
Get back
No home
Trio

Collecting dust
Cool in moonlight
Waiting on us
To get right.

Bo's Baptism

Dante was not my only little brother reborn
For the sun-soaked
Everlasting morning,
Smuggled out from under
Splintered Egyptian yokes,
Freshly transcribed
In the *Book of Life*.

Pastor delivers sermon
About submersion
As just symbolic
Of spiritual renewal and, yet,
Dante says he felt God's presence
Sure warmth
Saw light form
No power source.

Mother tongues up hallelujahs
By the baker's dozen,
Rejoices right through noon
And all night, too.
But, my other little brother, Bo,
Who opened eyes also
And saw all water,
Asked what I thought, so
I say,

Hell if I know, Bo.
Come on,
Dry off,
Let's go home.

Going home was a psalm,
An ocean,
Was a concrete step
Of a cracked back stoop,
Faded pocket bible
With my blue ink inscription
And a very special breakfast
Of eggs, pork sausage,
Potato fried real nice to split
And fit to twin.

Harlem Bird Watching

Watching Bird strut
On in the front,
Through the club,
Atop the bandstand,
Polished sax brass
In hand, I knew
One scandalous truth—
How I'd do
Near anything,
Everything,
To be his woman.

To have been that fly
On their gilded wall,
To have seen those
Blood-drained,
Nauseated faces
The moment
They got hip to it all,
What our love had done—
Their fair princess,
Done run amok,
And this [*luminous*]
Negro junky.

Some Men Should Never Have Had Children

Go 'head, asshole, keep
Your fucking money!

We wish you luck
But tell you this:

You better pray to God
That new woman croaks
After you do

'Cause if she don't
And it's just you,
Best get ready to go

One sad and lonely
Deadbeat motherfucker
And you know it's true!

Leaving Limbo

They let you go
'Cause they don't know
That bag you snatched
Absent compassion
Piss poor on plan
Only lowered shoulder
Like fist to chin thrown
Laid somebody's mama
On back of troubled bone
TKO cold comatose
Spilling precious yolk…

Well, she's dead now.

No joke?

Dreaming Hours

This is no time to worry about nothing
Now's the dreaming hour
And sure
They say we poor
But I keep that lamp on in the hall
Crack your door
So go on let big bad light bill
Soar high as it wants to fly
If we can always go shoot old crow down
From open window
With this here bow
'Cause neighbor lady
With ornery dog
Still owes me that spare arrow she borrowed
For something she won't tell
So I don't know
So leave that sorrow for sunny morrow 'cause, no

This is no time to worry about nothing
For now's the dreaming hour
And if you want that cup cool water
I'll fill it
And if the night isn't quiet enough
I'll hush it
And if that shadow grips your wrist
I'll expose it

And whatever you got
That you just can't drop
Well then home
They stole it
So free your tired child mind 'cause, no

This is no time to worry about nothing
For now's the dreaming hour
And dreams need sleep
Like fish need sea
And if we wanna big fish
Then we got to go deep
But not too far
Cause farther we go
Harder it'll be to breathe
And when you finally do rise
It'll be to pure sunshine
Light blue sky
Polyester suit, clip-on tie
But eggs and grits first
Cause another Sunday morning
So you know we're going to church
And I got just enough bus fare
To get us there
And we'll say prayers
For merciful return and, so, no

This is no time to worry about nothing
For now's the dreaming hour
And when they come
They go blind

But you see
How life wasn't real when you woke
Or honest if you're conscious
But we're not ripe for a chat like that 'cause, no

The Move

And a woman spoke, saying
Tell us of The Move
And I said:

A syncopated patter
Slow amplifies
Four sets Chuck Taylors
Causing collisions
Eight worn rubber soles
Smacking hot asphalt
Below heavy labored breath
Of run boy lungs
Quick siphoning oxygen
From city atmosphere.

And the cop car siren
That steel hooting owl
Or was it mooing cow?
Rooting sow?
Electric yawp echoed
From next block over
Talons tearing T-shirts
Clawing young backs
As prey emerges out
From a narrow alley.

Pelted patrol car
Well-dented door
Brick fragments
Shattered window glass
Still in lap, but
Not a single face to attach
To name
Number
Rough up good
Before booking.

Kid jukes down ditch
Hides quiet in drainpipe
Secure in rusty womb
Breathless
In a whale's belly.

You clever boy
Quick-visited by wisdom
Who won't stroke
Cold juvenile hall walls
This day.

To survive a childhood
Without margins
And, in time,
Sirens recede
Near silent
And this boy, half god,
Emerges out
With more juice than Jonah.

To a choir of Old Heads
Shit talkers recycling lies
Passing cheap wine down line
Of wooden crates
Who've seen it all before
But, rejoice:

There it is, y'all!

That's the move!

Jim Crow Guide
to Playing Hooky

We pinched our noses
We inhale and with

Lungs full enough to
Bust bellies, dove in

Past broke with eyes
Willed open

Racing toward
Reaching out for
Kicking

Blues bent toward
Basic black
But none of us ever
Truly touching
The muddy bottom
And so, at last, just

A little swearing aloud
A bit of splashing about

As if that mattered

Near deep as

Its living mysteries.

    ***

Off shirts, lost pants
Low branched

No socks, holed shoes
But,

No lessons and
No picking, see

We're here
Too busy

Gone swimming

With no reasons to run

We were
Skin glistening
Like God's son.

    ***

Much less preserved
In the ambers above

Than secured in love
Right where we was
Going where child
By decent whites won't
Then down

In those cool Nahs
Crisp Sorry, Sirs
And clean Ain't Seem 'Ems of

Our still waters.

Gigi's Food Truck

Thank you, Sir.
Yes, God bless

Our famous
Mobile soul
Food kitchen

Biggest platters
In the city

Earth trembling
Deep fried whiting
Jerk chicken
Peach cobbler
Beans and rice
Rice and peas
French fries
Collard greens
Veggie medleys
Oxtail stew
Yams
Plantains
Beignets
Banana pudding
Sweet potato pie
'Bout to make me cry.

Meat patty Mondays
Fried shrimp Fridays

Gumbo Sundays
If you're lucky.

Pick your meat
And 2 sides

Hands down best
Food you'll find
Rollin' thru here
On four wheels

Heaven w/ 2 sides

Take you there
On a two-way
Ticket.

Cornbreads etc.
Drinks in the cooler

No refunds
No refunds
But no refunds

And, sure, just now
Coming soon—
We cater.

So, what y'all want?

HUGHES

Jazzonia

(oh) Just a bit of silken gold in
Eve's cabaret eyes lifts (oh) six rivers. Jazzers play

of a gorgeous whirling
                      soul, a shining (oh) tree high.

The first garden was Cleopatra
                      singing, dancing in
                      a silver dress.

The shining cabaret soul   of Harlem jazzers: of
the long-headed tree, of   the long-headed rivers,

shining   silver   play. (oh)

a bold tree soul in (oh)
bold gown. Six rivers

were in a girl whose eyes are (oh)
                    too gold.

The Weary Blues

Heard a Black man's hands
Went all poor dead and then
Died in deep swaying

He thump the blues
With the blues,
Those weary blues he played
On piano stool
Down on that
The ebony avenue

He played his on each pale ivory fool
He sang a melancholy old foot
He put troubles
With melody

And nobody in this world-echoed night
Made that piano croon on more
To moon, stars.

I wish I had no few happy chords
To thump with a sad dull rock
But I can't be satisfied,
My playing on the shelf
And I got a drowsy syncopated rocking nobody got.
And by the pallor of light,

I ain't myself.

Back and forth, his lazy sway,
His lazy sway satisfied the rickety floor
I heard he got mellow
Like a man that's slept far into that tune.
Went to bed,
Tune to gas,
Weary moan
Droning through weary night.

The voice
The tone
That moan
I ain't quit coming from a thump.
A frownin' Negro play my sweet musical tune
While other singer crooned
And he did
And he did
Ain't got mo'

The blues stopped
The blues went out

O Blues!
O Blues!

The South

Syphilitic cotton for
a Negro's laughing

blood is a rare honey-
lipped love.

My South,

the lazy, scratching
mistress, she spits and

the Black children of
the South

escape her

cold-faced gifts. Who
with a spell, turns

my house, now the fire's
ashes upon

the cruel

Beast-strong earth. May
I say in child-minded black

face, "Is that its bones, so
beautiful magnolia-

scented woman?"

But, in the North, I am
a dark-eyed whore and

I am many. The kinder
North, seductive as

the sky,

they seek stars, but give on
back the sun and moon.

The South, the sunny-
faced South, her warmth

and her passionate

mouth, warmth for the
idiot-brained. The

South, who would like me
dead in her. The South,

she would.

Harlem

A just maybe
Explode it over
Dry meat

Or crust and sugar
Or load it up heavy
Then run rotten.

Sags, does it?
Or syrupy like?
Deferred?
And what does it stink like?
Like a raisin?

A sweet dream happens
In the sun
A sore does fester.

Nude Young Dancer

What night-dark boy have you hung, forest tree?
Have under what star-white moon?
What of your great bower?

What mother has under offered your midnight-hour lips?
What jungle has your veil?

The jungle tree of the jazzy swaying girl hips
Been like a sweet-slept perfume dancer.

You clean?
Have you slept about?

I, Too

When the company
Comes in, Darker

Brother,
Tomorrow comes, too—
Ashamed.

 "Send me to
America, too,"
They say.

But nobody'll dare laugh,
Sing, grow beautiful.

Kitchen company,
I'll eat, eat in.
Be kitchen table.

Besides, see how strong
I am, Brother?

I am well to me
And America.

They'll be.
When I am.

The Jester

Shall I be sorrow's hand? I hold masks.
Laugh, booted,
          booted.

                    You would laugh.

Black Jester
With me

The world with me in one tragedy—
And reign in the other.

                    Once, it was the pain

Dumb clown
Comedy

Tears at my
Grinning mouth.

               I am again wise.
               You are my laughter.
               Laugh at my laughter.

Wise fool of silly men,
Cry for my soul if you will weep.

Mother to Son

I'se climbin' up life and

fall

down on the crystal
boards, hard floors
torn

in the bare
honey light.

But, sometimes, ain't
been so
well for me and

I'se   still   you.

I'se been in dark
corners, no crystal

been on stair steps,
the landin's and

had splinters,
tacks.

'Cause, Boy, been

a-climbin'
for, reachin'

it, turnin'
with, goin',
and finds life,

it's   you,   too.

And it's still
goin' on.

Son, I'll tell you
kinder places

where you don't
turn back
for me

all the time and
don't, don't
you now!

And there ain't no
floor, landin's, no
carpet

ain't no
set stair.

Dream Variation

The quick day is in, at rest
Evening sun is then done. That is,
The coming of a cool
Black night.

Dance to tall, pale tree
While some whirl white into
A dark place and fling
Slim evening-arms wide
Like me.

My arms tenderly till,
Whirl at,
Fling wide,
Whirl of,
Gently rest beneath my dream.

My night dance,
'Til the tall sun comes on
Done like me, to the tree,
To face the day.

April Rain Song

The rain drops
the silver, a

night lullaby on
your head.

Let the rain

        rain.

     Let rain kiss
     the roof.

The rain pools
sleep in a song,
plays

   you upon
the gutter, makes

still sidewalk pools
sing on beat.

With love,

let the rain

rain.

You and I
our running   makes

      the little
      liquid.

When Sue Wears Red

Again   my heart wears an   ancient jones   is
like the red a   pain blast. Come by

with her from sharp time dead trumpets, a cameo in
                                        brown beauty.

Susanna Jones walks ages of red
                        love fire night.

When Susanna turned some face,
Jesus burns   silver.

Once, a queen of Egyptian trumpets in red wears and
when Jesus trumpets, sweet Susanna
                        jones the blow.

                        Jesus!

Fantasy in Purple

Let the death-
song whir

      for stormy, but

drown the slow
dying choir with

drums,
      one note of

blaring sun.

Let the trumpet
blow of a

      breath and beat

the tragedy,
my tragedy.

Beat
the drums,   the drums

to violins and beat

the white rattle
of tragedy

         to thin of

darkness.

Sing for me,

to me   and   of me
and go where

I go.

To a Little Lover-Lass, Dead

She

searched for the rim
of

her waif lips
in

the kiss and now,

his of an endless night
nothingness has

gone into
lonely day.

Sweetdeath walks
the quietway

the street to
God.

Still lovers were

like a dark land

    beyond.

        She gives

little.

        Who would?

Proem

I, the cut-off hands
               of Africa, carried
the Woolworth Building to
his doorsteps. Now,

they lynch a slave.

The clean black Caesar
                    I am, me, a Negro singer.

I brushed the black boots of
Washington

as my sorrow songs told me Texas made
the victim pyramids,

                         black like
the Belgians keep,
like the Georgia night
a ragtime black.

A black worker arose
          from under depths,
                    made to mortar in
my hand.

I've been Negro.
I've been Black.

"I, I, I've been of my Africa, the Africa.
I've been in the Congo all the way."

Night, I am depth.

Afraid

We are the skyscrapers
                    we cry among:
Africa in our palms
Ancestors
Night.

Cried among
And afraid because,
                    as it is,

                              we're alone.

Lenox Avenue:
Midnight

Cars laughing to the swish rhythm
                              of broken rain, the honey
      undertones
                of pain. The heart

rhythm of Lenox
                        Avenue is a midnight rumble,
        weary
                overtones of street

life. Gods love at the weary heart, at
                              the honey of us and
      (to us) the gods are
                    laughing the jazz.

Suicide's Note

Face the river

The kiss
          of cool

Asked me for
Calm.

The White Ones

Faces torture you; hate

                    strong ones. Me?

I do not hate beautiful
I do not torture loveliness,

                    splendor. Yet,

Why do you?
White do you?
Why are you?
And your faces,

           too.

O, whirling for me, too!

ALL CUT *UP*

From the Park

When I was young,
I sat in a diner with my father and witnessed.

They were in the park and nothing more
Conversation
They saw a chance to get their names

Unshackled.

History
Form history
And you can choose to remain anonymous.

The park and nothing more
A chance
First moment until now
Most amusing passage.

Had their attitude been absurd, rather than otherwise
Had their names been absurd
Rather than otherwise
We could have deliberately refrained from seeing

History
Burn history
Remain anonymous.

The *"anger in these young men"*

Unrelating form and matter
The pigmy matter, the people of New York
Negro ministers
Zoological Park
The whole episode
History, form, and the redress of real grievance
Names
Their names.

The pigmy matter, this incident, this ridiculous matter
Good comic-opera material
Dark meat, dark matter
This matter.

But none of them, they, the Negro ministers
Ever have seen the pigmy in a cage
Either as exhibit, in print, five-minutes seeking.

To give up the pleasure of a leisurely stroll in the park at dusk.

Dr. Verner's African pigmy
Newspaper sensation created
Most amusing passage.
They were in the park, nothing more
Saw a chance
And were advised to call upon me.

We have not yet heard who has him
Out of nothing

May have created
Out of nothing
Even when adjusted to himself.

In saying that they are serious, in the park and nothing more
Without annoyance or discomfort
Unrelating form, matter, pigmy
Most amusing Passage.

We are glad to learn that you have declined, Dear Mr. Mayor,
To seriously consider
Real grievance.

This justifies me.

When the will is written
We could have deliberately refrained from seeing:
Real grievance
False passage
The pigmy in a cage
They were in the park and in a cage
Names
And indignation
Newspaper
Their names.

Seeing him, a single person, seeing him
Names in a cage, in passage
Dr. Verner's very interesting little African
Passage in a cage,
Cage in Passage.

This episode will interest you.
They have a lawyer
And a view.

Mayor Koch has stated that hate and rancor should be removed from our hearts.
I do not think so.

Newspaper the alleged
Matter with a view.
That he was caged, part of their race, of the park
With this view
A lawyer with a view
In the times that be.
I have no archives to preserve;
I am enclosed with you.

I want them to be afraid.

Ota Benga has not been in a cage for several days.
He did not become the cage
Dictated on all points
Perfectly the label
Information confirmed by arms, hands
Shown flat
Subject in the cage.

You will continue with Mr. Grant on this foot
Imperative means *no take*
But Mr. Grant considers it quite untrue and we agree.
Have a conference and concur

Of course, you doubt
I hope you will.
Release him during the day
With this view
Mornings only for a month.

To remove the boy, not even seen
To keep him here, so hard to manage
The boy has to be read entirely:
From his cage
Set in paper
As an exhibit, innocuous, destitute, sure—

The park
Nurturing society
Rather long read
Nevertheless, as a matter of fact,
Fallen
Take down
Do not believe anything you pray by force.
Entire colored race
Browbeaten with a view
To sustain us.

This is not about Ota Benga.

The Negro head in form, in Passage,
I asked if it was true north.
Telephone said, "Yes, send him along at once."

To have control of the pigmy would be quite useless

Unless they can own him
I told him.
To have him flat
Right there
Whenever you so wished
To fulfill some distorted inner need
To know only his void
I demanded, Drop—
Further
Further
More
Approve
Agree.

I am not looking to psychoanalyze or understand them.
I am looking to punish them.

The pigmy stands (situation here ...)

Refuse, rethink
Unruliness brings risk of possibility.
Make him hard to control
An attitude.
Take care to see me
Not Ota Benga at all
Paper
Matter on condition
Trouble in form
I do not believe the situation here in accordance with your wishes.

Of course, I know a proper person.

Was useless.

To pursue, to take without serious trouble
Coming after him
Anxious to own
Their own vicious brand of hatred
Our only hope for relief
And why do they laugh?

I am sure subject
Presence, reason, status.
The newspapers have made so much
But we must give it
Our man
Our names
Our form
Everything told
Away.

Surrender the boy absolutely and for all time.
"We just wanna talk to 'im..."

You will appreciate this point
Take after him for this
Willing a warm Carolina morning
Would be possible
Thought to save himself
To take your asylum
Not Ota Benga at all.

Be wise to offer that and so much

I am not that—
The idea, the African, yours, thanking you
I think it would not be all theatre.
I beg pigmy to remain at the party.
Mr. Grant has not replied.
The pigmy has you now.

Whether to carry out unwelcome events for your kind.

At the Zoological Park it is proposed
To give him good supply of insurmountable
Upon which to exercise his manual skill.

Quarters will remain genuine.

Coal black rivers married
Locality was confluence
Kasai and Sankuru
Ota, tributaries, time
Captive in the hands of every afternoon.

His height is 4 foot 11 inches;
He is 23 years old.
Convey him back to his own
He will be back again—equatorial
Black, though not what is.

Quarters will remain genuine.

Explorer and collector—
Mr. Verner's cannibalistic necessities

Met and described under various names no one can say.
America, the great failed home,
Quite expert in the making of words
No one can say.

Scattered communities will remain genuine.

He can be seen during work hours
At the Primate House
Accompanied by a fine young chimpanzee
Good head
Bright eyes
Pleasing.

This explorer decided to give him this attempt to return passage,
The complete breakdown of life as we know it.

When I was young,
I sat in a diner with my father and witnessed

Men and women of that race stolen
Men and women of that race died
Not found
Now on exhibit temporarily, genuine, flat
In the ape collection
At the Primate House.

Little man with a poisonous snake, chrome-plated
The fear of retribution
The bite of a very well formed word
No one can say.

MOVE: RESOLUTION NO. 200609

introduced October 29, 2020

WHEREAS,   immeasurable
enduring harm
sanctioned   May 13, 1986; and

WHEREAS,   recklessness in
              and conflict   part
                          MOVE

                  and following the tragic
        Osage Avenue; and

WHEREAS,   failed
                pain   Family
        ; and

WHEREAS,
        force   mirrors   force   6221 Osage
                ; and

WHEREAS,   end~~uring~~
                    deaths   five   six

- Netta Africa, age 12,
- Tree Africa, age 14,
- Phil Africa, age 11,
- Delisha Africa, age 12,
- Tomaso Africa, age 9,
- John Africa,
- Conrad Africa,
- Raymond Africa,
- Frank Africa,
- Rhonda Africa, and
- Theresa Africa

on May ~~13~~, 1985; and

WHEREAS,   61 homes
        6200 block   ; and

WHEREAS,

                                their homes

        Osage   ; and

WHEREAS,   harm
                  a result   official
orders issued   ; and

WHEREAS,

              Bombing; and

WHEREAS,   echoes

       shaped   between police and   ; and

WHEREAS, The uprisings   ~~around~~   in the wake

George Floyd, Breonna Taylor, Ahmaud Arbery, David Jones and ████

today; and

WHEREAS,   towards

past; and

WHEREAS,   day of

wounds   this day
happening again; now, therefore,

RESOLVED,

the spirit   moving.

FURTHER RESOLVED,   Africa
████████   this   body.

AFTER*WORD*

Electric Sliding for a New World

You can't see it
Stony the road we trod

You gotta feel it
Bitter the chastening rod

You gotta know it
God of our weary years

Now, you can't hold it
God of our silent tears

But you know it's there
Here, there and everywhere.

Some say it's mystic
Have not our weary feet

You can't resist it
Yet with a steady beat

You can't do without it
Facing the rising sun

Don't want to lose it
Of our new day begun

But you can't choose it
True to our native land

But you know it's there
Here, there and everywhere.

I've got to move
Full of the faith that the dark past has taught us

I've got to groove, groove, groove
Full of the hope that the present has brought us

Are you comin' with me?
Over a way that with tears has been watered?

And I'll teach you, teach you, teach you
Treading our path through the blood of the slaughtered

But you know it's there
Here, there and everywhere.

You can't see it
Stony road trod

You gotta feel it
Chastening rod

You gotta know it

Weary years

Can't hold it
Silent tears

But you know it's there
Here, there and everywhere.

Some say it's mystic
Weary feet

Can't resist it
Steady beat

Can't do without it
Rising sun

Don't lose it
Day begun

Can't choose it
Native land

You know it's there
Here, there and everywhere.

Got to move
Dark past taught us

Got to groove, groove, groove
Present brought us

Comin' with me?
Tears been watered?

I'll teach you, teach you, teach you
Blood of slaughtered

Know it's there
Here, there, everywhere.

No, you can't see it
That stony road trod

So, you gotta feel it
That chastening rod

So, you gotta know it
Those weary years

No, can't hold it
Them silent tears

Yet, you know it's there
Here, there and everywhere.

And some say mystic
Our weary feet

But y'all can't resist it
That steady beat

Can't do without it
That rising sun

Can't lose it
Our day begun

And, no, couldn't choose it
Our native land

Still, it's there
Here, there and everywhere.

And, still, we movin'
Full of the faith that dark past taught us

And, still, we groovin', groovin', groovin'
Full of that hope the present brought us

And, still, you comin' with?
That way with tears been watered?

Well, then, I'll teach, teach, teach you
Treading path through blood of slaughtered

'Cause, you know it's there

Here, there, everywhere

notes

The poems within Section Two, **Hughes**, are word re-organizations. The corresponding source poems were originally published in Langston Hughes' 1926 collection, *The Weary Blues*.

"From the Park" contains found language lifted from two sources: the correspondence records concerning the kidnapping and imprisonment of Ota Benga recently made public by the Bronx Zoo, and Trump's 1989 full-page newspaper ad, advocating for the reinstatement of New York's death penalty (to execution the Central Park Five).

"MOVE: Resolution No. 200609" contains found language lifted from a 2020 resolution passed by the city of Philadelphia, formally apologizing for the 1985 police raid and bombing of the MOVE collective on 6221 Osage Avenue.

"Electric Sliding for a New World" contains found language from two songs: "Lift Every Voice and Sing" and "Electric Boogie."

reading guide

Theme: **Found language as a tool of kinship and/or resistance**

Like musicians, a poet can sample different kinds of source texts towards a number of different ends. A text historically used toward violent or destructive ends can be turned against itself, repurposed to support healing. A text intended to sow isolation and distrust can be reworked to build kinship and connection. In addition, texts already intended to build connection and community can be reimagined to create new, dynamic forms of connection.

Representative Poems:

- "Electric Sliding for a New World" (pp. 90)
- "From the Park" (pp. 71)
- "MOVE: Resolution No. 200609" (pp. 80)

Theme: **From the margins: time, memory and the archive**

If one abandons the notion of linear time, how might this change our relationship to the past? What was once considered the past is no longer passed, never gone, but woven into our present moment. When applied to the freedom struggles of marginalized peoples and communities, often excluded from dominant historical narratives, the reclamation and reimagining of one's history bears a subversive potential, challenging the archive's claims to legitimacy and truth.

Representative Poems:

- Any poem from the Hughes section (pp. 42–67)
- "La Mott Community Gardens at Midnight" (pp. 15)
- "Jim Crow Guide to Playing Hooky" (pp. 35)
- "Bo's Baptism" (pp. 24)

Theme: **Musical traditions as radical traditions**

As both an art form and mode of communication, marginalized peoples and communities have used music to convey potentially subversive ideas and meanings. In this sense, the creative process itself can act as a demonstration of freedom. Improvisation--rule setting, bending and breaking--elevates to a practice for the affirmation of one's being.

Representative Poems:

- "Betty Carter Poem" (pp. 17)
- "Strange Fruit" (pp. 12)
- "Slow Drag in B/E Misdemeanor" (pp. 21)
- "Paper Cicadas" (pp. 8)

Theme: **Anti-Blackness, death, and rupture**

In Christina Sharpe's *In the Wake: On Blackness and Being*, she writes, "The ongoing state-sanctioned legal and extralegal murders of Black people are normative and, for this so-called democracy, necessary; it is the ground we walk on. And that it *is* the ground lays out that, and perhaps how, we might begin to live in relation to this requirement for our death. What kinds of possibilities for rupture might be opened up? What happens when we proceed as if we *know* this, anti-blackness, to be the ground on which we stand, the ground from which we attempt to speak, for instance, an 'I' or a 'we' who know, an 'I' or a 'we' who care?" In this way, if anti-Blackness is and always will be inseparable from American democracy (and we engage with this fact), what truth must we speak, for what purposes, and how are we to speak it?

Representative Poems:

- "Sketching Lesson" (pp. 5)
- "Kitchen Table Séance" (pp. 3)
- "Leaving Limbo" (pp. 28)
- "MOVE: Resolution No. 200609" (pp. 80)

acknowledgments

Thank you, God.

Thank you, J. K. Fowler and the entire Nomadic Press crew, for your confidence, support, compassion, and integrity.

Thank you, Michaela Mullin, for your generous and invaluable editorial guidance.

Thank you to the faculty, students and alumni of the San Francisco State University MFA Program.

Thank you to the editors and staff of *Fourteen Hills: The SFSU Review* for extending to me your appreciation and community.

Thank you, Zenya Prowell, for your friendship. Thank you, Dasha Bulatova, for your timely support and encouragement.

Thank you to my amazing family: to my mother, for moving heaven and earth for me; to my father, for his inspiration, groundedness and strength; to my sister, for her love, inspiration and vision; to my brother, for his real deal 24-7 all around flyness; and to my two nephews, for bringing light to even the most challenging of times. Thank you to all my kin, immediate and extended, here and gone, for providing the creative heart of this book.

Thank you to my wife, Alivia, for your brilliant and abundant love.

KEITH DONNELL JR.

Keith Donnell Jr. is a Philly-born, Bay Area-based poet and book editor. He earned his MA in English at the University of Southern California and his MFA in Creative Writing at San Francisco State University. He was a previous Editor-in-Chief of *Fourteen Hills: The SFSU Review* and his work has appeared in journals and anthologies, most recently *Puerto del Sol, Cagibi, Jubilat* and *Best American Nonrequired Reading*. He lives in Seaside, California, with his wife, Alivia, and two cats, Ember and Mika. This is his first book.

cover missive

On "Cover art: costume worn by Nona Hendryx of Labelle (designed by Larrry LeGaspi)"

By the Author, Keith Donnell Jr.

Afrofuturism is a scholarly and/or aesthetic practice of imagining a more liberated future for Black people. The idea is that this imagining entails a reimagining of our present moment—a practice meant to inform how we live our lives *right* now. In the 1970s, all-female soul/funk/rock singing group, Labelle, incorporated this aesthetic into their music and performances. The cover of this book presents one such stage costume.

OTHER WAYS TO SUPPORT NOMADIC PRESS' WRITERS

In 2020, two funds geared specifically toward supporting our writers were created: the **Nomadic Press Black Writers Fund** and the **Nomadic Press Emergency Fund.**

The former is a forever fund that puts money directly into the pockets of our Black writers. The latter provides up to $200 dignity-centered emergency grants to any of our writers in need.

Please consider supporting these funds. You can also more generally support Nomadic Press by donating to our general fund via nomadicpress.org/donate and by continuing to buy our books. As always, thank you for your support!

Scan here for more information and/or to donate.
You can also donate at nomadicpress.org/store.